FIRST Picture Words Book

Hindi & English BOOK
FOR BILINGUAL CHILDREN

All rights reserved. No part of this publication may be reproduced, distributed, or transmitted in any form or by any means, including photocopying, recording, or other electronic or mechanical methods, without the prior written permission of the author.

फल (phal) Fruit

सेब (seb)

apple

नाशपाती (naashapati)

pear

केला (kela)

banana

स्ट्रॉबेरी (strawberry)

strawberry

नारंगी (narangi)

orange

अंगूर (angoor)

grapes

फल (phal)   Fruit

चेरी (cherry)

cherry

नींबू (nimbu)

lemon

ब्लूबेरी (blueberry)

blueberry

नारियल (nariyal)

coconut

आड़ू (aadu)

peach

अनानास (ananas))

pineapple

फल (phal) Fruit

कीवी (kivi)

kiwi

आम (aam)

mango

तरबूज (tarbuj)

watermelon

अंजीर (anjir)

fig

आलूबुखारा (alubukhara)

plum

रसभरी (rasbhari)

raspberry

सब्ज़ी (sabzee) Vegetable

कद्दू (kaddu)

pumpkin

प्याज (pyaaj)

onion

कुकुरमुत्ता (kukuramutta)
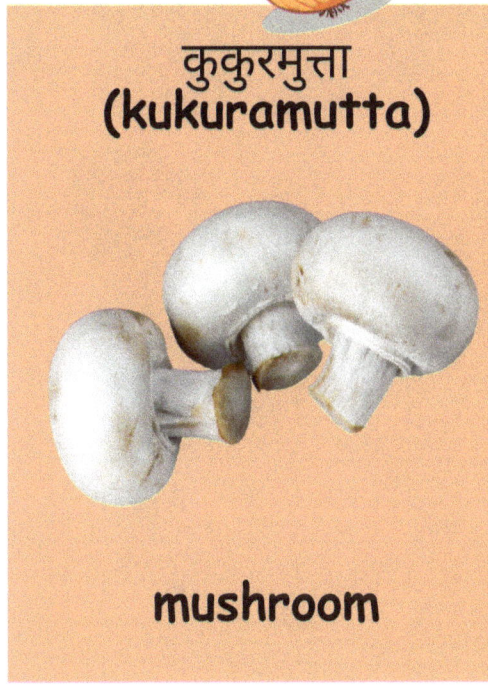
mushroom

खीरा (khira)

cucumber

पत्तागोभी (pattagobhi)

cabbage

टमाटर (tamatar)

tomato

सब्ज़ी (sabzee) Vegetable

बैंगन (baingan)

eggplant

आलू (aaloo)

potato

फलियाँ (phaliyaan)

beans

फूलगोभी (phoolgobhi)

cauliflower

मूली mooli)

radish

ब्रोकोली (broccoli)

broccoli

सब्ज़ी (sabzee) Vegetable

लहसुन (lahsun)

garlic

सेलेरी (seleri)

celery

गाजर (gajar)

carrot

चुकंदर (chukandar)

beetroot

भुट्टा (bhutta)

corn

शलजम (shaljam)

turnip

खाना (khaana) Food

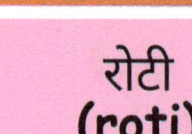
रोटी
(roti)

bread

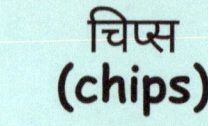
चिप्स
(chips)

chips

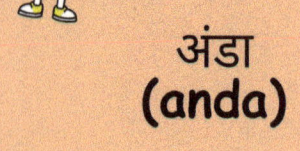
अंडा
(anda)

egg

दूध
(doodh)

milk

पेनकेक्स
(pancakes)

pancakes

गोश्त
(gosht)

meat

खाना (khaana)   Food

बर्गर (burger)

burger

सलाद (salaad)

salad

पास्ता (pasta)

pasta

पिज़्ज़ा (pizza)

pizza

शोरबा (shorba)

soup

नूडल्स (noodles)

noodles

खाना (khaana) Food

मक्खन (makkhan)

butter

बन (bun)

bun

जाम (jaam)
jam

पनीर (paneer)

cheese

चटनी (chatani)

sauce

चावल (chaval)

rice

खाना (khaana) Food

केक (cake)

cake

आइसक्रीम (icecream)

ice cream

पुडिंग (pudding)

pudding

दही (dahi)

yogurt

डोनट (donut)

donut

कुकी (cookie)

cookie

खेत के जानवर
(khet ke jaanavar) — Farm Animals

गाय (gaay)

cow

कुत्ता (kutta)

dog

बिल्ली (billee)

cat

भेड़ (bhed)

sheep

मुर्गी (murgee)

hen

सुअर (suar)

pig

खेत के जानवर
(khet ke jaanavar) — Farm Animals

बत्तख (batakh)

duck

बकरी (bakri)

goat

हंस (hans)

goose

खरगोश (khargosh)

rabbit

घोड़ा (ghoda)

horse

गधा (gadha)

donkey

जंगली जानवर
(jangalee jaanavar)
Wild Animals

शेर (sher)

lion

हाथी (hathi)

elephant

बाघ (bagh)

tiger

भेड़िया (bhediya)

wolf

तेंदुआ (tendua)

panther

भालू (bhalu)

bear

जंगली जानवर
(jangalee jaanavar) — Wild Animals

जिराफ़ (jiraf)

giraffe

ज़ीब्रा (zibra)

zebra

बंदर (bandar)

monkey

साँप (saanp)

snake

कंगेरू (kangaroo)

kangaroo

पांडा (panda)

panda

जंगली जानवर
(jangalee jaanavar) — Wild Animals

लकड़बग्धा (lakadabagdha)  hyena	गिलहरी (gilhari)  squirrel	प्लैटीपस (platipus)  platypus
हिरण (hiran)  deer	चूहा (chuha)  rat	लोमड़ी (lomadi)  fox

कीड़े (kide) Insects

मधुमक्खी (madhumakkhi)	मकड़ी (makadi)	मक्खी (makkhi)
bee	spider	house fly

तितली (titli)	चींटी (chinti)	भृंग (bhring)
butterfly	ant	beetle

समुद्री जानवर
(samudri janvar) — Sea Animals

कछुआ (kachhua)	केकड़ा (kekada)	अश्वमीन (ashvameen)

turtle	crab	seahorse

व्हेल (whale)	तारामछली (taramachhali)	डॉल्फ़िन (dolphin)

whale	starfish	dolphin

समुद्री जानवर
(samudri janvar) — Sea Animals

सील (seel)	ऑक्टोपस (octopus)	जेलीफ़िश (jellyfish)
 seal	 octopus	jellyfish

शार्क (shark)	मछली (machhali)	वालरस (valaras)
 shark	 fish	 walrus

पंछी (panchhi) Birds

उल्लू (ullu)

owl

चील (chil)

eagle

तोता (tota)

parrot

मोर (more)

peacock

हंसावर (hansavar)

flamingo

पेंगुइन (penquin)

penquin

वाहनों (vahanon) Vehicles

रेलगाड़ी (relgadi)

train

कार (kaar)

car

साइकिल (saikil)

bike / bicycle

बस (bas)

bus

विमान (viman)
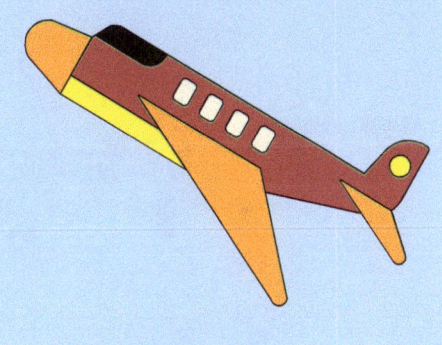
plane

जहाज़ (jahaz)

ship

वाहनों (vahanon) Vehicles

एम्बुलेंस (ambulance)
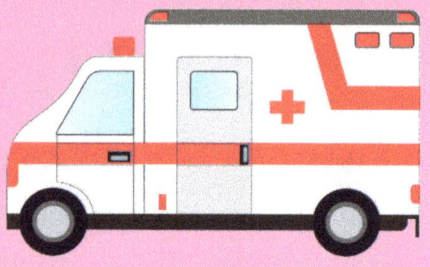
ambulance

रॉकेट (rocket)

rocket

नाव (naav)

boat

मोटरसाइकिल (motorcycle)

motorcycle

ट्रक (truck)

truck

हेलिकॉप्टर (helicopter)

helicopter

खिलौने (khilaune)   Toys

गुड़िया (gudiya)

doll

गुब्बारे (gubbare)

balloons

गेंद (gend)

ball

पतंग (patang)

kite

टेडी बियर (teddy bear)

teddy bear

खिलौना ट्रक (khilauna truck)

toy truck

रंग (rang) — Colors / Colours

लाल (laal) — red	नीला (neela) — blue	हरा (hara) — green
पीला (peela) — yellow	धूसर (dhusar) — gray / grey	गुलाबी (gulabi) — pink

रंग (rang) Colors / Colours

काला (kaala) — black	बैंगनी (baingany) — purple	भूरा (bhoora) — brown
नारंगी (narangi) — orange	सफेद (safed) — white	चैती (chaiti) — teal

जगह (jagah) Place

पार्क (park)

park

पाठशाला (pathshala)

school

पुस्तकालय (pustakalaya)

library

चिड़ियाघर (chidiyaghar)

zoo

खेत (khet)

farm

समुद्रतट (samudratat)

beach

जगह (jagah) Place

दुकान (dukan)

shop

अस्पताल (aspatal)
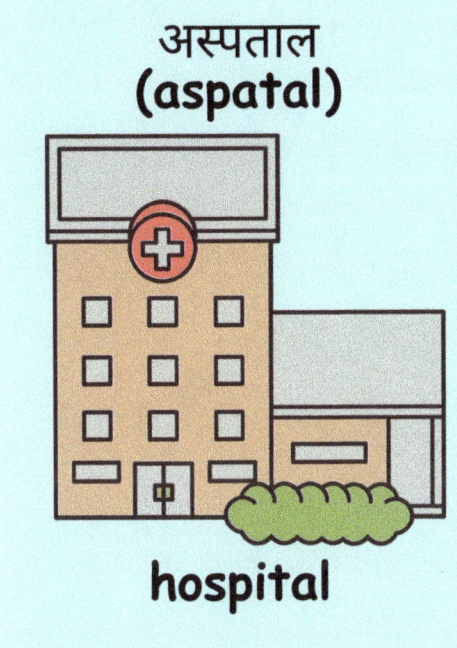
hospital

भोजनालय (bhojanalay)

restaurant

पूल (pool)

pool

कक्षा (kaksha)

classroom

स्टेडियम (stadium)

stadium

प्रकृति / बाहर
(prakriti / bahar)
Nature / Outdoors

सूरज (sooraj)	चाँद (chand)	सितारे (sitaare)
sun	moon	stars

इंद्रधनुष (indradhanush)	ग्रह (grah)	बादल (badal)
rainbow	planet	clouds

प्रकृति / बाहर
(prakriti / bahar)
Nature / Outdoors

पेड़ (ped)

tree

फूल (phool)

flower

समुद्र (samudra)

sea

पौधा (paudha)

plant

सीप (seep)

seashells

पत्ता (patta)

leaf

प्रकृति / बाहर
(prakriti / bahar)
Nature / Outdoors

आसमान (aasman)	सड़क (sadak)	जंगल (jangal)

sky	road	forest
चट्टान (chattan)	स्लाइड (slide)	झूला (jhoola)

rock	slide	swing

मौसम (mausam) Weather

धूप (dhoop)

sunny

हवादार (havadar)

windy

बादल छाना (badal chana)

cloudy

तूफ़ानी (tufaani)

stormy

बर्फ़ीला (barfila)

snowy

बारिश (barish)

rainy

घर (ghar) Home

घर (ghar)

house

बैठक कक्ष (baithak kaksh)

living room

भोजन कक्ष (bhojan kaksh)

dining room

रसोईघर (rasoighar)

kitchen

गैरेज (gairej)
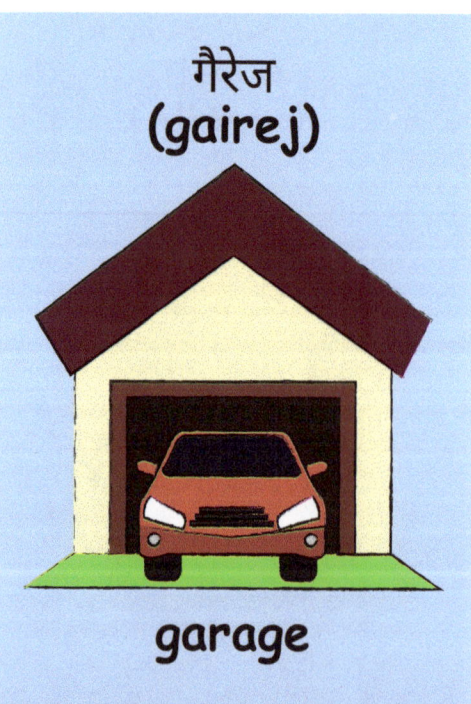
garage

स्नानघर (snanaghar)

bathroom

घर (ghar)   Home

शयन कक्ष (shayan kaksh)	अटारी (attari)	लॉन्ड्री (laundry)

bedroom	attic	laundry
घर कार्यालय (ghar kaaryaalay)	नर्सरी (nursery)	आंगन (aangan)

home office	nursery	yard

घरेलू सामान
(gharelu saman) — Household Items

दरवाजा (darvaja)

door

बिस्तर (bistar)

bed

घड़ी (ghadi)

clock

कटोरा (katora)

bowl

तस्वीर (tasvir)

picture

छत (chhat)

roof

घरेलू सामान
(gharelu saman)
Household Items

खिड़की (khidki)

window

अलमारी (almari)

cupboard

कुर्सी (kursi)

chair

मेज़ (mez)

table

प्रकाश बल्ब (prakash bulb)

lightbulb

परदा (parada)
curtain

घरेलू सामान
(gharelu saman) — Household Items

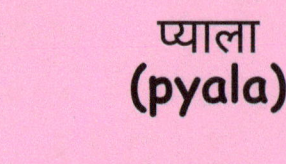
प्याला
(pyala)

mug

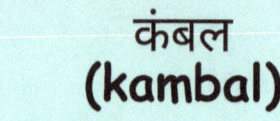
कंबल
(kambal)

blanket

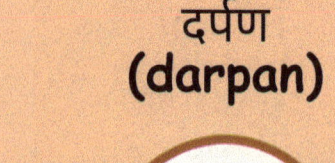
दर्पण
(darpan)

mirror

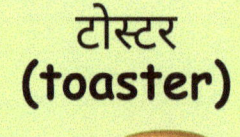
टोस्टर
(toaster)

toaster

नल
(nal)

tap

किताब
(kitab)

book

घरेलू सामान
(gharelu saman) — Household Items

गिलास (gilaas)

glass / tumbler

थाली (thali)

plate

कांटा (kanta)

fork

टोकरी (tokari)

basket

चम्मच (chammach)
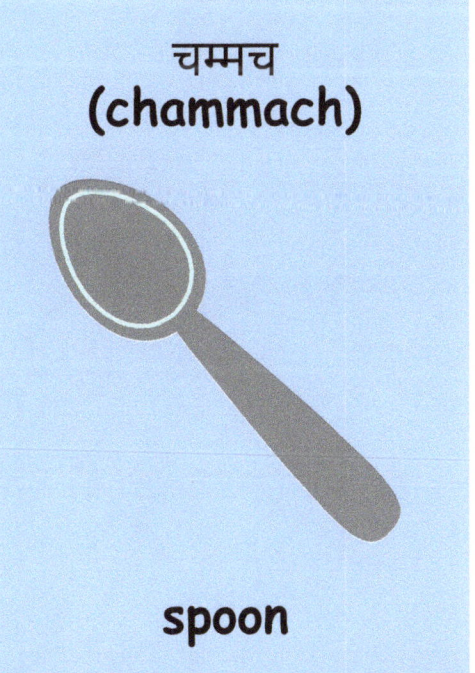
spoon

चाकू (chaku)

knife

घरेलू सामान
(gharelu saman) — Household Items

पंखा
(pankha)

fan

टॉर्च
(torch)

flashlight / torch

चाबी
(chaabee)

key

कैंची
(kainchee)

scissor

तकिया
(takiya)

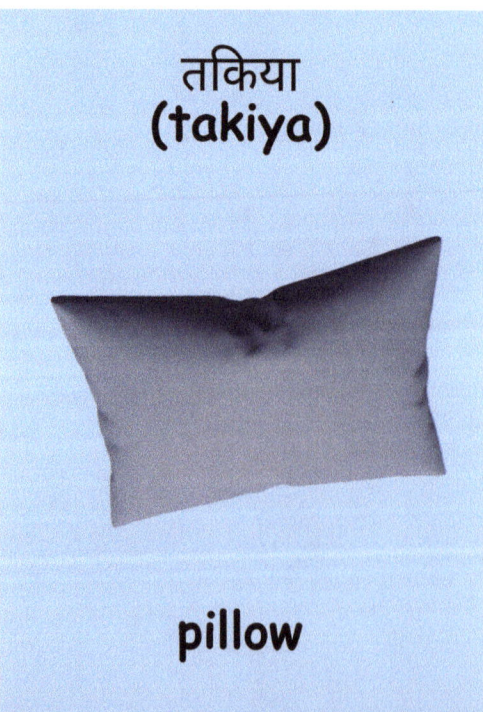

pillow

पेंसिल
(pensil)

pencil

घरेलू सामान
(gharelu saman) — Household Items

कंघी (kanghee)

hairbrush

छाता / छतरी (chhata / chhatri)

umbrella

स्टूल (stool)

stool

सीढ़ी (sidhi)

stairs

मटका (mataka)

pot

केतली (ketalee)

kettle

मज़ा (maza) Fun

स्नान (snan)

bath

ब्रश (brush)

brush

खेल (khel)

play

खाना (khana)

eat

पढ़ना (padhana)

read

नींद (neend)

sleep

मज़ा (maza)　　Fun

चलना (chalna)  walk	लिखना (likhna)  write	नाचना (nachana)  dance
गाना (gonna)  sing	पीना (peena)  drink	तैरना (tairana)  swim

लोग (log) People

माँ / माता (maa / maata)  mom / mother	शिशु (shishu)  baby	भाई (bhai)  brother
बहन (bahan)  sister	पिता (pita)  dad / father	शिक्षक (shikshak)  teacher

लोग (log)   People

दादी / नानी (daadi / naani)

grandma

दादा / नाना (daada / naana)

grandpa

लड़की (ladki)

girl

लड़का (ladka)

boy

चिकित्सक (chikitsak)

doctor

दोस्त (dost)

friends

कपड़े (kapade)   Clothes

जूते (joote)

shoes

कमीज (kameej)

shirt

टोपी (topee)

hat

स्कर्ट (skart)

skirt

पोशाक (poshak)

dress

पंत (pant)
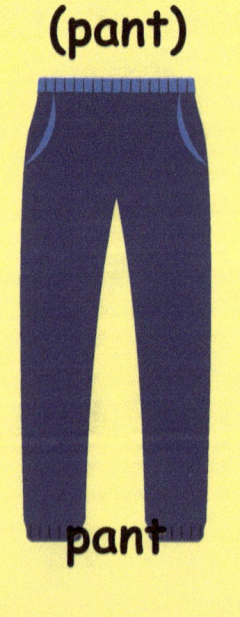
pant

कपड़े (kapade) Clothes

जम्पर (jumper)

jumper

मोजे (moje)

socks

दस्ताने (dastane)
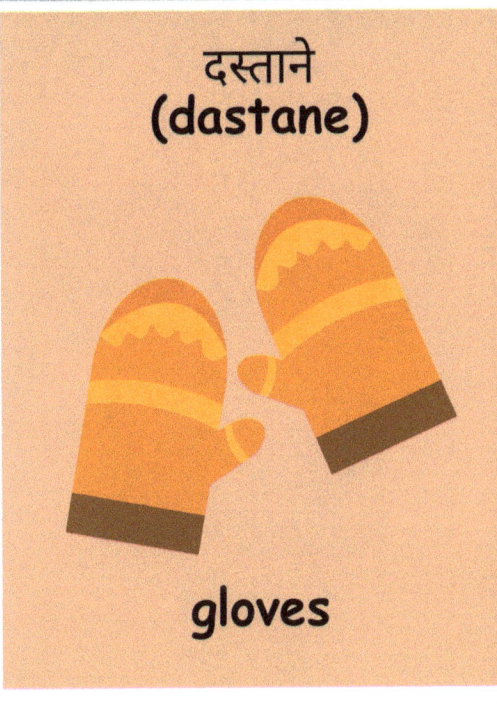
gloves

निकर (nikar)

shorts

बेनी (benee)

beanie

जूते (joote)

boots

कपड़े (kapade) Clothes

टी शर्ट (t shirt)	चप्पल (chappal)	टोपी (topi)
	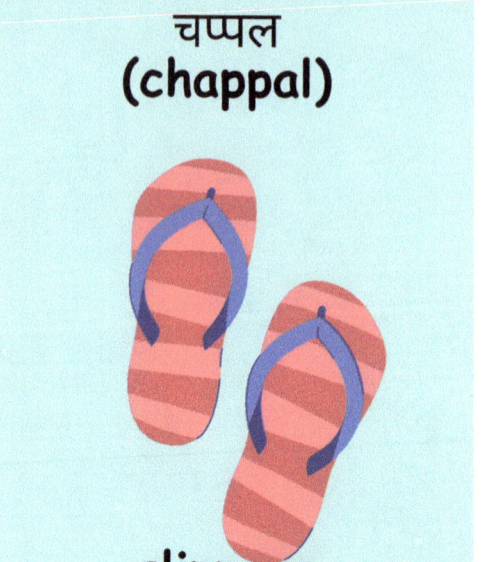	
t-shirt	slippers	cap
मफ्लर (muffler)	कोट (coat)	टाई (tai)

scarf	coat	tie

शरीर (shareer)   Body

आँख (aankh)	कान (kaan)	नाक (naak)
	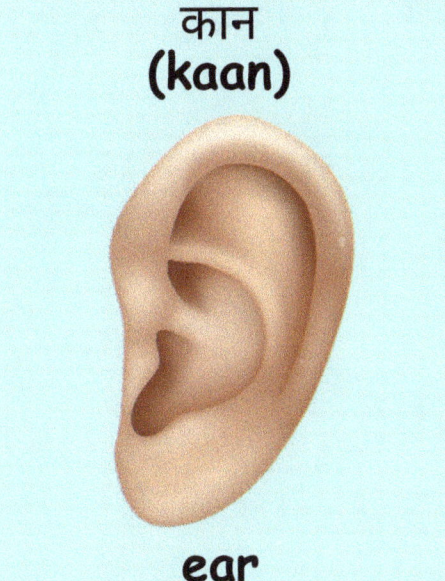	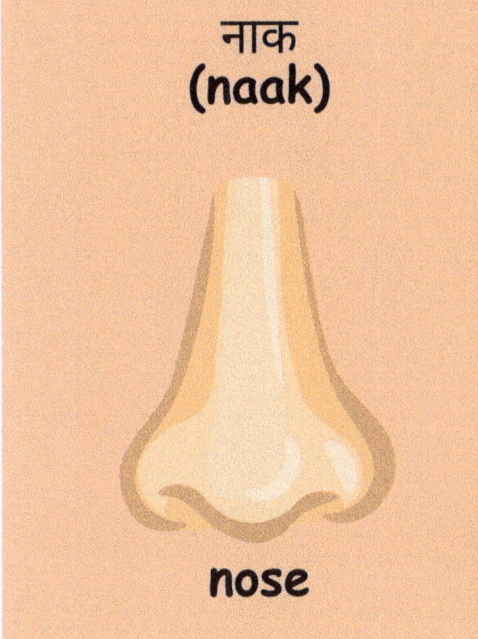
eye	ear	nose
चेहरा chehra	मुँह (muh)	दांत (dant)
	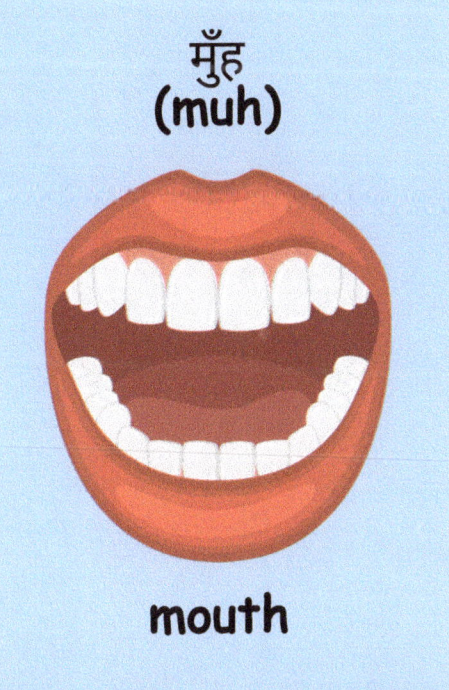	
face	mouth	teeth

शरीर (shareer) Body

ठोड़ी (thodi)
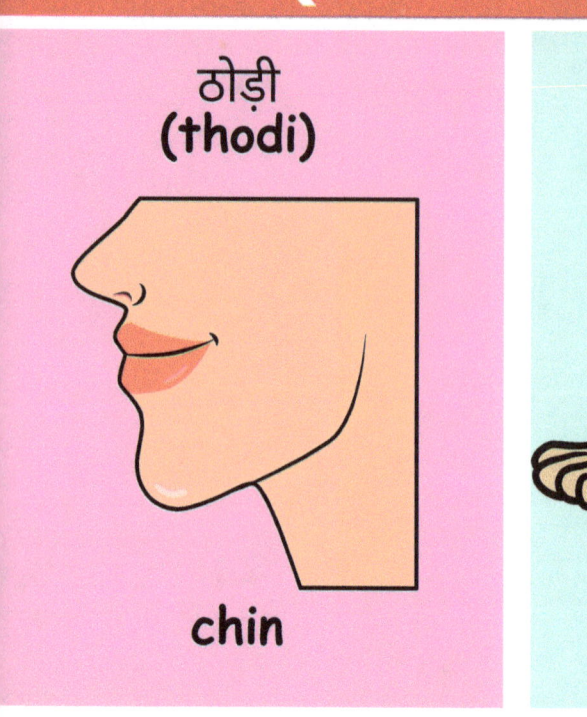
chin

पैर (pair)
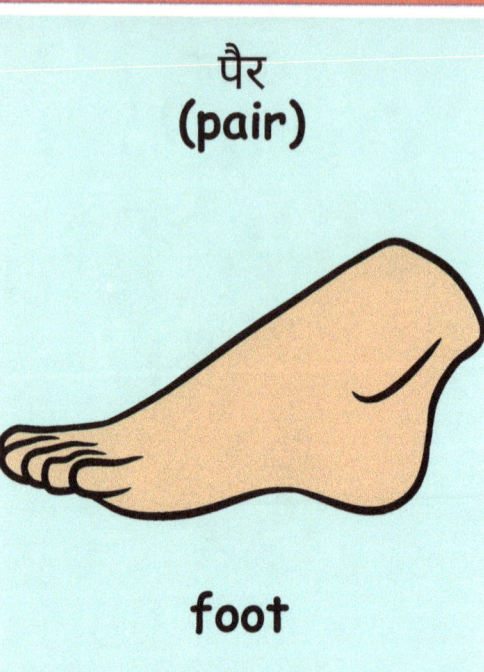
foot

गर्दन (gardan)
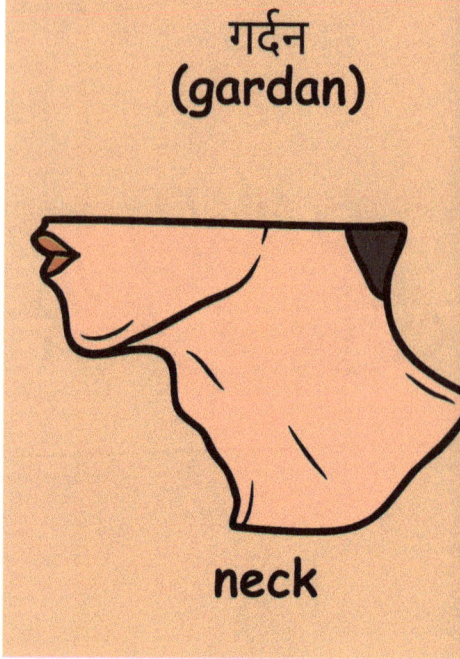
neck

हाथ (haath)
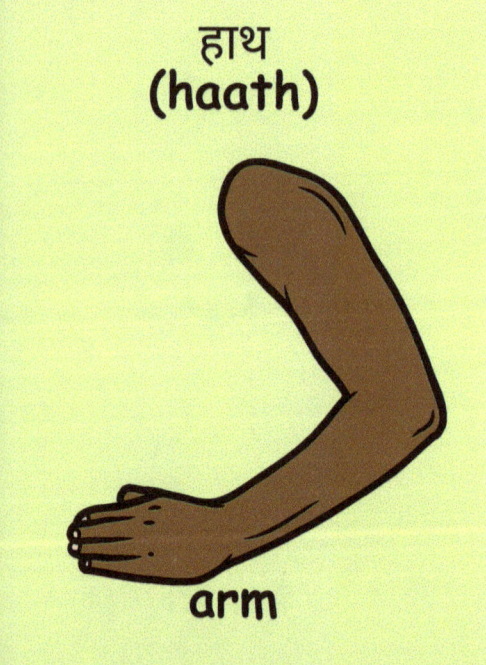
arm

हाथ (haath)
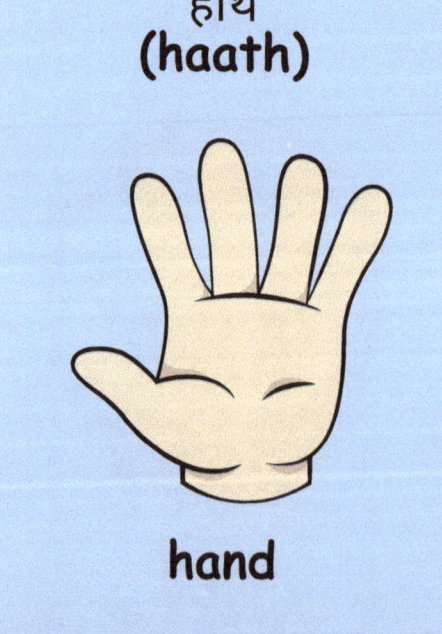
hand

पैर (pair)
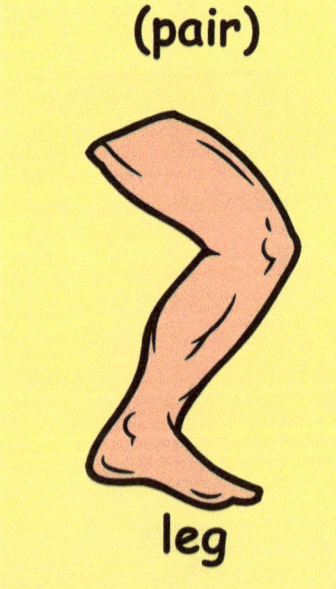
leg

आकार (aakaar) Shapes

चक्र (chakra)

circle

वर्गाकार (vergakar)

square

त्रिकोण (trikon)

triangle

आयत (aayat)

rectangle

पंचकोण (panchakon)

pentagon

अंडाकार (andaakaar)

oval

संख्या (sankhya) Numbers

एक
(ek)

one

दो
(do)

two

तीन
(teen)

three

चार
(char)

four

पांच
(paanch)

five

छह
(chhah)

six

संख्या (sankhya) Numbers

सात (saat)

seven

आठ (aath)

eight

नौ (nau)

nine

दस (thus)

ten

ग्यारह (gyarah)

eleven

बारह (barah)

twelve

Dear Readers,

Thank you for joining us on this adventure and for reading our book. Creating books for children is a joy and a privilege, and we are grateful for the opportunity to share this with you.

Creating and writing a book is a labor of love, and it would not be possible without the support of a community of people who believe in your work. Thank you for being a part of that community, and for making this book possible.

As a small business, every customer is important to us, and thank you again for choosing to read our book. If you liked this book, please support us by leaving a review.

Best regards,
Kidzikki Bookz

www.ingramcontent.com/pod-product-compliance
Lightning Source LLC
Chambersburg PA
CBHW061134010526
44107CB00068B/2940